I Pray They Serve Henny In Hell

RAFAEL WILLIAMS

DEDICATION

- To everyone that ended up in it in this book. You, unwillingly, participated in moments of my life that made me who I am today.

- To my Mother. Please don't disown me after you read this. As a matter of fact, don't read this, put the book down!

- To the maker of the Plan B pill. If it wasn't for, you my child support payments would have consumed me by now. Lord knows my condoms have broken a few times.

- To the authors before me. Thanks for paving the way and never suing people.

DISCLAIMER

The stories you are about to read are 100% true. A few names have been changed to protect the innocent and save a few feelings from being hurt. However, a lot of names were not changed because, I really don't fuck with those particular individuals any more. I know, I know, they are still people with feelings. So, here we go. Here's my blanket apology. If you are a guy and I tell an embarrassing story about you catching an STD or shitting on yourself because you can't hold your liquor, my bad. If you are a woman and ended up in this book as result to us having sex, I'm sorry. On another note, if you are a woman that I had sex with and didn't end up in this book, maybe you need to step your game up in the bedroom. Nobody sue me! Enjoy the book...

When you sit with a nice girl for two hours, it seems like two minutes. When you sit on a hot stove for two minutes, it feels like two hours that's relativity.

-Albert Einstein

When you're in some good pussy for two hours, it seems like two minutes. When you sit on a stove for two minutes, it feels like two hours that's relativity.

-Bob Oblaw (What Einstein wanted to say)

CONTENTS

Dedication   i

Disclaimer   ii

Introduction   1

Humble Beginnings   4

Rafael Beats Up A Seven Year Old Girl   21

The Pissing Girl   38

Beef With The Jamaican Mafia   48

Rafael Becomes A Pimp: Part I   60

Rafael Becomes A Pimp: Part II   79

The Crying Game   95

Rafael Receives Rapture   113

About The Author   131

INTRODUCTION

First of all, thanks for purchasing this book! Unfortunately, you have just been scammed. The rest of the pages are blank! I'm just joking. Within these pages lie eight of the most entertaining, comical, and true stories you will ever read. Truthfully, you may want to hurry up and finish reading because; I've already been offered a sitcom spinoff based on the book. This may ruin it for you when all of your co-workers are talking about the latest episode. Ok, I'm lying but, it's a damn good book.

If you have sensitive ears here's a fair warning, there is a lot of foul language in this book, all sorts of awkward situations, and I think me and Jesus get drunk somewhere in here. Look, here's an easy fix for your sensitivity, when you see a curse word imagine it says, "BEEP." This is exactly what everyone else in the world does when censors place beeps in movies. We imagine the beep is actually the curse word that was removed. It's a win-win for everyone. Ok, back to the book.

This book probably has a few grammar errors. I mean commas and shit might not be where they need to be. A word or two might be spelled wrong. It's cool! Just make a mental note of the discrepancy then, when you write your book, don't make that mistake. Ha Ha Ha. I'm just playing; it's all in fun bruh.

If you're reading this book then you've obviously seen the title. You might have even read books with similar titles. Some of you may argue that the writing style of this book may be similar to other books. Take it as me paying those authors homage. I'll tell you one thing though; all these stories are 100% factual! So, Disregard the fact that you may have purchased this from the fictional section of the book store and enjoy the read!

HUMBLE BEGININGS

At age 13, I was raped. Now, before you go imagining somebody sticking a dick in my ass, know this, I was raped by a woman. You're probably like, what the fuck? How is that even possible? Newsflash motherfucker, women do rape men! Especially when you're as sexy as I am. But, before I get ahead of myself, allow me to start from the beginning. Oh and I apologize for calling you a motherfucker. I mean, you did buy my book. But, I digress.

It was the summer of 1999. I ran with a group of hard heads by the names of Brandon, Roderick, Eric, and Rodney. These motherfuckers got me into more shit than I care to remember. Pause. Just so you know I curse a lot. Ok, back to the story. Where was I? Oh yeah. These motherfuckers got me into more shit than I can remember. Honestly, I'm surprised I'm not locked up right now. A perfect example; I remember one late afternoon, I was leaving the basketball court.

Brandon asked me, "Where you going, Raph?"

Without skipping a beat I replied, "Home bruh, Fresh Prince bouta come on." This was the reason I used but, every nigga on that court knew the real reason I was leaving. Yep, you guessed it. The street lights were coming on. Back then this was the universal signal for kids all over the world to take they ass home. Unfortunately, I was the last one in my little clique that still had to follow this rule.

Brandon said, "Fuck that, enough is enough. You staying out tonight. Fuck them street lights!"

I looked Brandon in the eyes, looked at Rodney, threw my basketball at Roderick, pushed Eric and hauled ass. They chased me down and grabbed me. I cursed, yelled, and threw as many uppercuts and jabs as possible but, I could not escape. I could hear my momma screaming, "Rafael!!!!! Get your ass in this got damn house!!!!" Obviously, she didn't hear me screaming for help.

After about 30 minutes, they finally let me go. Out of breathe, pissed off, and scared my momma was gonna beat the black off my ass, I walked home. When I got there my prediction came true, I got the ass whipping of a life time. After this epic beating, I tried to explain to my mother that my friends held me down because I was the only one that couldn't stay out pass dark. I hoped she would hear how I was getting picked on and decide to give me an actual curfew. But, that didn't happen. She told me to get new friends. My momma didn't play!

Despite my friends being the reason I was always in trouble, I still hung out with these guys daily. As boys transitioning to men, we only had one thing on our minds that summer and that was sex. Every day we would chase girls hoping to get them into our beds, in the back of a car, on side of a house; hell, anywhere we

could get 3 minutes of privacy with a girl, we were
trying. But the truth of the matter was, none of us had
ever had sex. This was soon about to change. The first
one to fuck a chick was Rodney. He was a year older
than the rest of us so, this made perfect since. Next,
was Brandon then Roderick then Eric. It was official; I
was the last one in the clique to still be a virgin. Even
Eric got some pussy and he was uglier than a mother
fucker. I mean this nigga was so ugly, at birth his
momma originally named him "Shit Happens". He was
so ugly, as a kid he had to trick or treat by phone.
Despite the fact of his ugliness he had done something
I hadn't, he had sex.

Every day after they broke their virginities, they
bragged on it. I mean every day. Finally, it was
apparent; I was the only one not talking about
fucking! Rodney was the first to realize this and he
started to clown me. Now there's something you have
to understand about my particular group of friends.
These dudes were ruthless. Imagine Bernie Mac,
Martin Laurence, Richard Prior, and D.L. Hugley all
cracking jokes on you simultaneously. This went on

for weeks I was called everything from "The little virgin that could" to "That gay nigga that wasn't fucking nothing." I was even called the Virgin Mary for two days. My friends told everybody I was a virgin. I remember one time we were playing basketball with the older kids in the hood and Rodney called a timeout.

Eric looked baffled. "Damn Rodney, why you called a timeout? We winning?"

Rodney bowed his head. "We need to take a moment of silence for all the virgins on the court!"

Everybody looked around, confused.

Eric smirked. "Raph the only virgin on this court."

They all laughed! I'm talking over 20 upperclassmen that I would be going to school with next year, including my cousin Tyrell.

Now, Tyrell was my favorite cousin. I looked up to him. He was a 17 year old playa and a scholar. He could pretty much get any girl he wanted to. He was well known for fucking the baddest bitches in the school! Unfortunately, I found out he was gay nine years later. But, I'll save that story for another chapter. What happened next? Oh yeah.

With a look of disgust on his face, Tyrell asked, "Nigga you a virgin? Ain't no cousin of mine bouta be no fuckin' virgin."

I shouted, "Man, fuck no I ain't no virgin. I fuck all the time."

With a smile on his face, Tyrell asked, "Who you fucked?"

Lost for words, I did the only thing I could think of, I lied on my dick! Yep, I picked a pretty girl we all knew (Latonya Morris) and told them I had sex with her. Pause! Shout out to Tonya. My bad Tonya, I didn't mean to lie on you and I didn't mean to put your name in my book but fuck it, it's in the past now. Anyway, back to my story.

Tyrell, trying to hold on to the street cred he created, smiled and said, " I told y'all my cuz wasn't no virgin."

We wrapped up the longest timeout ever and finally finished the game. After we were done ballin', my cousin was still on his high horse. He talked about almost every girl he fucked trying to cover up my virgin embarrassment with his own accomplishments. These accomplishments included Rodney's older sister. I found this particularly enjoyable. Tyrell's boys were still harping on the fact that my friends called me a virgin.

One of them said, "You might be fucking but, yo cuz not."

Tyrell jumped in quick screaming, "My cuz ain't no virgin. In fact, him and his lil homeboys are coming with us on the Southern University tour next week. We gonna smash every chick there."

Now, this tour was intended for high school seniors only so, I was confused. But, as soon as Rodney heard the invite, he jumped in screaming, "Shit yeah we coming."

I whispered to Rodney, "chill out bruh."

He looked back at me mumbling, "Man it's gonna be a shit load of bitches there."

Two weeks later we were on our way to Southern University. Pause! Where the fuck is the rape story? Hold your horses my favorite reader; the rape story is almost here. Ok, back to the nitty gritty. We took a bus to the college. You want to hear something fucked up? This trip was sponsored and chaperoned by our local Baptist church. They put this trip on every year and every year when the old church folks fell asleep, the dorms became a giant orgy! This was pretty much the main reason everyone signed up. Once we arrived to the college; we had a little orientation, checked into our dorms, then ate the complementary meal they provided. So far, I was good and no one was even talking about sex. This was the case until about 9:30pm.

Tyrell pulled out a bottle of vodka. It was passed around to a few people then, the conversations started. Tyrell and his friends had already devised a plan to sneak into the girls section of the dorms. It was probably the most genius idea a 17 year old has ever had. It didn't involve climbing through windows or coming down a chimney. It was (drum roll please) simply to knock on the door. Can you believe this shit? Tyrell suggested 10 boys just walk up to the girl dorms and knock? I went along with it and guess what, this shit actually fucking worked.

Now we were sittin in the female dorms, passing a bottle of vodka around and trying to get in one of the girl's bed. I think one of the girls there said she was a virgin or something because suddenly, the conversation was steered to me.

Rodney said, "Oh yea? My boy Raph a virgin too."

You remember them old hood parody movies when a white guy walks into an all black club and the music comes to a screeching halt? I swear that shit happen right then and there. Everybody looked at me in disbelief .

Tyrell came to my defense, "My cousin ain't no virgin. We discussed this already."

Rodney chuckled. "Then who he fucked? Because, it damn sure wasn't Tonya. I asked her."

Tyrell squinted his eyes and stared in my direction, "Cuz you fucked her right?"

"Hell yea I fucked. Rodney don't know what he talking about."

Rodney screamed. "Bullshit, I know what I'm talking about because, I fucked last weekend. When I heard you fucked, I thought it would be easy so I took my shot. At first she didn't wanna give me no play. So, I cursed her out and asked why she let yo' ugly ass hit. After I said that she went off talking bout you ain't never hit and you never will."

I jumped in, "Nigga you lying. I know I fucked."

Rodney pulled out his phone. "Well let's see."

Oh shit! He was calling Tonya. My bluff was about to be called! Let me remind you, this was all done in front of everyone that was in the common area of the female dorms. He put the call on speakerphone so everybody could hear.

Tonya answered. "Hello."

"Hey Tonya, this is Rodney. I got a question for ya. Did you let Rafael hit? Because, he standing right here telling everybody he did."

She went off! "Fuck no I aint let that little skinny motherfucker hit. And he better stop telling people that or I'm gonna make my brother whip his narrow ass."

The room got silent for a second then erupted in laughter.

Tyrell screamed. "Everybody shut the fuck up before I start whipping some ass in here."

Everybody piped down because they knew he meant it and really could take everybody in that room.

Tyrell walked over to me. "You breaking your virginity tonight."

He got all the ladies attention. "Who gonna break my cousins virginity tonight? Somebody better step up or I'm taking my liquor back to my room."

This 18 year old stallion started to smile. Ok, she really wasn't a stallion and her face looked like the bottom of an old pair of Jordan's but, she said, "I'll do it. He's cute."

Tyrell smiled. "Keep the party going." He ushered me and the girl into a vacant room. Pause! I know this is fucked up but, I can't remember this girls name to save my life. All I remember is she is from Farmerville, Louisiana. So, if by any chance you know a girl from there that is ugly with glasses but, had a banging body back in 1999, tell her I said what's up. But again, I digress. Tyrell ushered me and Farmerville girl into an empty room. My heart was jumping out my damn chest. I was shaking and nervous. I was actually about to have sex for the first time!

Tyrell opened the door to a vacant room. "Yall don't come out this room until y'all finish fucking." Then he closed the door.

Farmerville girl leaned in to kiss me. I pulled back. Not because I was scared but, because she was kind of ugly and the number one rule back then was not to kiss girls. Kind of contradictory I know but, this is how we rolled.

Farmerville girl said, "Look baby, if you're scared or nervous just tell me and we will just chill in here for a while. After a few minutes we'll walk out and you can tell your boys we fucked."

I said, "Cool." Because truthfully, I was scared as hell.

Farmerville girl told me a bit about herself. She told me that she was struggling with the decision to attend Southern University or Grambling State University. These were the two major black colleges in Louisiana. I told her I was probably going to go to Southern. After about 15 minutes of talking I calmed down.

Suddenly, Tyrell popped his head into the room. "Y'all niggas ain't fucking yet!?! Raph, you better take those damn pants off and fuck that girl before I beat yo' ass in here." Then he looked at Farmerville girl. "And don't think I won't fuck a chick up!" Fucking peer pressure bruh, I swear!

After he closed the door Farmerville girl looked at me. "You heard yo' cousin. Take them pants off. That nigga crazy."

I was confused. "I thought you said we were just gonna chill and then leave."

"Boy take them pants off before that nigga come in here and whip our ass. Would you rather get some pussy or get beat up and clowned by your friends?"

I would rather have gotten beat up. I was scared as shit but, I took my pants off. She took hers off then climbed on top of me. All I could think of was the fact that I had no condom and I couldn't have this ugly broad being my baby momma.

"I don't have a condom." I Said.

"Stop making excuses and be a man." She said.

She grabbed my dick and shoved it in her. Suddenly, all my butter flies went away. I was having sex! And it felt fucking amazing!!! I thought jacking off was the shit but, this was a million times better. After about five minutes we were done.

So, that's the story of how I was raped at 13. Not what you expected I know but, it's the fucking truth. Rape is uninvited sex right? I didn't invite that shit. So, it was rape. Sure once I got started I was addicted but, it's the beginning that matters. We soon left the room as I walked out all my boys, Tyrell's boys, and her home girls were standing outside the door. I had over 20 people cheering me on as I walked through the hall. The moral of the story is. My childhood was crazy so, when I say I'm a product of my environment, I mean exactly that. It's this foundation that made me a womanizer, gigolo, pimp slash playa, and most of all, a fucking SEX GOD. And it's also this foundation that set the stage for one of the best books you will ever read. Fasten your motherfucking seat belt and get ready for some crazy ass stories!

RAFAEL BEATS UP A SEVEN YEAR OLD GIRL

At age 22 I beat up a 7 year old little girl. Pause! Now before you go blowing this out of proportion or throwing this amazing book in the trashcan, you have to let me explain. It was the fall of 2007. I remember because, I had just celebrated my 1 year anniversary, of divorce. Yep, I was married folks. It's probably hard for you to imagine me being married but, I was. I was married to a beautiful (crazy), independent (crazy), and intelligent (fucking nuts and crazy) woman. Do you get where I'm going with this? Why did I get divorced you may ask? Did I get caught cheating? Nope, I never got caught. Did I lose my job? Nope, I actually got a raise. Then what you may ask? Well in the words of my uncle Jericho, "You show me a bad bitch, and I'll show you a nigga that's tired of her shit." Do you want to know what really happened? I wish I could tell you but my divorce decree prohibits me from going too deep into details. Ain't that some shit though? That shit is literally on my fucking divorce decree. "Rafael Williams will not taint the name of..." WTF! I'm not allowed to talk bad about my ex-wife. I thought that's what you suppose to do? If I wasn't scared I would get sued for every penny I have, I'd write a chapter on that shit too! Then I'd photocopy some old family photos (Polaroid's) and put them on the cover of this damn book. But, what would that accomplish? Anyway, where was I? Oh yea, I was celebrating 1 year of freedom. I wanted my first year anniversary to be special so I took myself to the best anniversary, of divorce, spot in Phoenix Arizona. Yep, you guessed it, the strip club!

My favorite strip club was called the Shitty Titty. This wasn't the real name of the strip club but, everyone called it that because the strippers were pretty shitty! So why would I go there? Cheap Hennessey! Two bucks a shot and five dollar lap dances. I would get two girls to dance on me at one time. Two fives equal a dime right? I arrived there early on my anniversary of divorce, to pregame with this guy I met at work named Kevin. Kevin had also been through a divorce recently so we had a shit load of celebrating to do. Now, Kevin was that loud drunk. You know the one that takes one shot then tries to fight the biggest nigga in the club. Despite this, they loved him in this club. He knew every shitty stripper by name and was even cool with the owner. I remember one time; they let him DJ half the night. They probably would have let him DJ the whole night but, he threw up in the DJ booth and ruined an eight hundred dollar turntable set. I think that was the night he was banned. After the club closed he broke in and stole all the alcohol. We had Henny for months! But hold up! This story isn't about Kevin. It's about me! So where was I? Oh yea, celebrating my anniversary.

I arrived early that night to pregame with Kevin. He was taking his sweet time getting there so, I just hung out at the bar. I wasn't drunk enough to get a lap dance from these homely looking strippers just yet so, I struck up a conversation with the new bartender.

"Hi", I said, "My name is Brandon." Pause. Brandon was the name I told girls in the club. Just in case they turned out to be crazy. Un-pause.

She replied, "Hi sweetie what can I get cha'."

We made eye contact. Now, my real players out there know this to be true. Talking to a chick is all about the vibe. If you feel that vibe you shoot your shot. When we made eye contact I felt that vibe. So, I replied, "Let me get a double shot of Hennessey and your phone number."

The bartender shook her head. "Wow, you're not even gonna ask my name? Not gonna happen buddy."

I clearly wasn't drunk enough and misread that vibe. No love lost. Kevin got there a few minutes later. The place was dead so, we took another shot and set course for Amare Stoudemire's night club.

When we got there the line was wrapped around the building. We tried to give the bouncer a twenty to get in a little quicker but, they weren't having that that night so we had to wait. We finally got in and it was epic! Women everywhere! Unfortunately, there were dudes everywhere too. The competition was thick! Luckily, I devised a sure fire method to eliminating 80% of my competition in any west coast club. It's called, "The Dougie Approach." Step one of this method is to analyze my competition. If the competition seems to be a majority of west coast men, ages of 20-26, this will work flawlessly. Step two; I approach the DJ, to make a song request with a 20 dollar bill in hand. Step three; I hand the 20 dollar bill to the DJ (he won't ignore you if you hand him money before make your song request.) Step four; request the most popular west coast dance song. An example of this is anything "Hyphie or Dougie" related. How will this eliminate your competition? Easy my friend. It's a well known fact that 98% of west coast men can't resist getting in a circle and dancing with each other. They dance battle, pop-n-lock, dougie, get hyphie and any other nonsense you can think of.

Now how does this help eliminate the competition? Allow me to explain. Once the DJ plays that first dance song the club will ignite with energy. Men from everywhere will make their way to the center of the dance floor. This will alert any DJ to keep that rhythm going. The DJ will be forced to play more songs that are similar to the one you requested. Before you know it 80% of the men in the club will be dancing with each other in the middle of the dance floor. So where are all the ladies? They are on the outskirts of the club starting to sit down deciding if they are going to Waffle House or IHOP after the club. This is when you make your move. Genius, I know!

That night it worked like a charm! I saw a group of ladies sitting at a table by the exit. They were looking bored and as if they were about to leave. I went in for the kill. I started the conversation with something honest that I know they can relate to.

"Hi ladies," I said, "My name is Brandon. Can I sit with y'all for a second?" They looked at each other for approval so, I continued to talk. "I hate when these niggas start dancing together. They pretty much ruin the club."

The prettiest one in the group replied, "Sure you can sit, I hate that shit too. It happens every time."

"What's your name?" I asked.

She said, "My name is Brittani with an "I" and I'm 7 years old."

So, I punched that bitch in the face because she had to be an alien or something! I'm joking. Just seeing if you were still with me. Back to the story. I said, "Well, Miss Brittani with an "I," am I treating you to Waffle House or IHOP after this?" Pause. This is a little known fact. If the girl says waffle house you're probably going to have sex with her. Waffle house girls enjoy life and chances are high, to get lucky.

IHOP chicks, on the other hand, are stuck up, so you may have to put in some work. If there is still time left in the night, abort and try someone else. Ok, un-pause.

Brittani said, "Neither, I have to get home to my kid."

Mission failed! Time to jump on one of her friends before it was too late to salvage the night. Right when I was about to switch to my secondary target, she uttered the two sweetest sentences a man looking for a one night stand could possibly hope to hear.

"You can come with me to my house so we can keep our conversation going. But, you have to keep it down my daughter's sleep."

I replied, "No problem, I don't even like loud noises."

Booty Call!!! I love booty call hours. You get straight to the point. No talking, no watching wack ass movies, no pretending to be interested in her dreams and goals, just straight unadulterated sex! I told Kevin to catch a cab home then, I left with Brittani. The night was everything I thought it should be. When the sun came up she made it easy for me.

"I'm not trying to kick you out or anything but, I have a lot to do today."

What! Have I found the perfect woman? It was too soon to tell. We continued our sexcapads for the next couple of weeks. It was the bomb.com, the perfect arrangement. She would text me about 8:30pm and ask if I wanted to kick it. I would reply yes or no. Then she'd tell me what time I should come over. I'd spend the night then leave around 6am so that I could go get ready for work. I told you, perfect fucking arrangement! But, after about 2 months I can see she was starting to fall in love with me. It was probably because I possess a magic penis. Pause. I would not be putting anything in this book unless it could be collaborated. My penis is indeed magical. Half the women on my face book page can corroborate these claims. But anyway, I digress.

One Saturday Brittani texted me around 2pm. I was confused. This was not the arrangement. "Damn you magical penis!!!! You are a gift and a curse," I yelled. Hesitantly, I replied with a simple smiley face text back. Women love smiley faces. She asked if I wanted to meet her in the mall for lunch and maybe catch a movie. I was literally headed up there because; I was bored out of my mind sitting in my condo. Condo? Condo, apartment, tomat-toe, tomatdo. Who's writing this?

Anyway, I was bored sitting in my CONDO and was literally headed to the mall when she asked me to go. Now Brittani was a beautiful girl so there was no reason I couldn't be seen with her in public. Plus, I was bored as fuck. I texted her back, "Sure lets catch a movie.☺" Got to have them smiley faces. I'm telling you, women love that shit. When I arrived to the mall she was already eating in the food court. Side Note: you don't invite someone to go eat and then eat before they get there. That's just plain ol' rude! But, at least I didn't have to pay for it so, that made it even out.

"So Brittani," I asked, "What movie do you want to see?"

"Paranormal Activity."

I heard mixed reviews about this movie. Some people said it was a good horror film, and others complained that production sucked and it wasn't scary at all. I don't normally watch scary movies or dramas with women. I don't need a chick seeing me scared or emotional but, today I made an exception. We got tickets for the 3:30pm showing. Brittani looked extremely happy. She had this radiant glow. Uh oh, she was glowing, she wanted to spend time with me, she was all happy and shit? I had to ask.

"Brittani", I mumbled, "Are you pregnant?"

She chuckled, "No silly, why would you ask that?"

"Because you got this look and you're acting too happy to be going to a movie."

She then went on to explain that her sister was in town for the weekend and offered to babysit her daughter. Normally she didn't let her sister babysit her daughter because she was a pot head but, she hadn't had a day out in so long and just wanted to get away. That made perfect since. I kind of felt good that I didn't blow her off, seeing how much this date meant to her.

We watched the movie. It had its parts but, it wasn't really that scary. As we left the movies, I still wasn't 100% sure she wasn't pregnant so, I asked her if she wanted to get a drink. Pause. This is a good method to see if your girl suspects she's pregnant. Ask to take her out for drinks. If she thinks she's pregnant she'll turn you down because she knows it may affect the baby. I call it my "at home pregnancy test." Ok, un-pause. We went to a bar close to her house for a few drinks. Truthfully, we had more than a few, we got fucked up! I probably should not have driven the few blocks to her house but, I did. And why you may ask? Because, drunk sex is the shit! When we got back to her house it was pretty late. We went straight to the bedroom. I laid her on the bed, pulled off her clothes and went Yabba Dabba Doo in that pussy! Yes, this means I made the bedrock! Remember, I do have a magical penis. I put her to bed then I started to dose off myself.

Now, do you recall the statement I made earlier? You know the one about paranormal activity not being too scary. Well, I was fucking wrong! I started hearing noises. Sounded like people outside trying to get in. I kept looking at Brittani thinking she was going to turn into a monster or something plus, I was drunk so, this shit was amplified by ten. I put my head under the comforter and closed my eyes. I was telling myself, "Rafael, stop acting like a bitch. You a grown ass fucking man." Well, I was actually saying, "Brandon, stop acting like a bitch. You a grown ass fucking man." Got to stay in character! I finally started to drown out the paranoia and get some rest.

Around 3am I awoke to a screeching noise. I figured it was my mind playing tricks on me again so I elected to ignore it. But this noise got louder! This shit had to be real. You can say I was acting like a bitch all you want to but I was shitting on myself. I slowly took my head from under the blanket. I swear I saw a demon. I tried to convince myself I was tripping but, the screeching sound was not going away. I sat up in the bed. I saw a shadowy figure in the doorway. I could barely make out the shadowy figure because it was very dark. The only light was the soft moonlight trickling through Brittani's wooden blinds. From what I could make out this demon looking thing stood 4 foot tall and had horns sticking up from out of its misshapen skull. I closed my eyes in disbelief but, when I opened them the demon was closer, approaching me and screeching louder.

I shook Brittani and whispered, "Bae, wakeup you got fucking monsters in your house."

She just moaned and rolled over. This caused the demon to get pissed. It bellowed the most frightening screech I've ever heard. This made me scream, "WHAT THE FUCK IS THAT!!!!!!" That little demon monster thing raised its hands to me and tried to attack. I cocked back my right hand and hit the demon so hard I dislocated my pinky. It flew across the room.

The ruckus woke Brittani. I had already started grabbing my car keys. I said, "Fuck the clothes, you can have that shit. You got fucking demons in yo' damn house. I'm outta here." I was shaking like a prostitute in church. Perplexed, she turned the lights on.

"HOLY SHIT!" Brittani screamed. "WHAT THE FUCK DID YOU DO TO MY DAUGHTER?" Yep, it was true. I had just knocked out a 7 year old little girl. I completely forgot she had a daughter. Here's my defense America. I've never met the little girl, I only came over after 9pm and I left before 6am each visit, she never spoke of her daughter, I was a bit tipsy from earlier, we watched a scary ass fucking movie a few hours prior, and it was dark. Now here's the kicker.

Have you ever seen a little black girl when they wake up in the middle of the night? Their hair is literally sticking up all over their head. As the moonlight hit this particular girl's head, I mistook her hair for little horns. The screeching, well, that was just the little girl whining for her mother. It was me that provoked the girl by cursing so loud. When she went to jump in the bed, I just followed my instincts. I feel bad about it but, that's the story of how I beat up a 7 year old little girl.

I convinced Brittani not to press charges by explaining to her what I thought I saw. She didn't talk to me for a good month but eventually, she let me hit it again. I just couldn't go to her house. One more thing, when I was leaving her house, after beating up her daughter, I felt pretty bad about myself. I was walking to my car when I smelled the sweet aroma of Mary Jane. It had been ages since I'd partaken in the stickiest of the icky so, I chose to follow my nose. There was a cute little chick smoking underneath the breezeway. I told her my name was Rafael and I just had the craziest night every. I offered her 20 dollars to smoke with her. She said, "Come on." She ended up giving me a blowjob under the breezeway outside of Brittani's house. That's fucked up I know. But, what makes it worse is that it was Brittani's little sister. And that's the story of how I got head outside of Brittani's house, after beating up Brittani's 7 year old daughter, by Brittani's 19 year old sister. You can't make this shit up!

I PRAY THEY SERVE HENNY IN HELL

THE PISSING GIRL

At age 23 I had a girlfriend that had a pissing problem.
I'm not talking about some freaky shit in the bedroom.
I'm talking about straight up pissing on herself in
random ass places. What?!? Yes, I felt just like that
the when I found out. I would think to myself, maybe
she has a condition or maybe she just drunk a lot of
water? Or maybe, the bitch just sprung a leak. I don't
know what the problem was but she clearly had one.
Let me start from the beginning and you can judge for
yourself.

In 2008 I dated a girl named... Wait! Should I put her
on blast? If you've been reading this book up to this
point then, you know I'm about to put that ass on

blast! Her name was Jade and she attended a state university. I met Jade at a college party in Arizona. I would say the name of the college but, I'm still a little confused on what I can say in books and what I can't. A nigga not trying to get sued. But anyway, Jade was a stone cold fox. She was a 5'10 redbone with legs that went on for days. The night I met her I swear I fell in love. Our conversation started out normal. You know, the standard bullshit niggas say when they are trying to get at a new chick. I told her how accomplished I was, I dropped hints about the type of car I drove, I may have even mentioned I was finishing up my PhD in the fall. Who knows, I was drunk as hell. Whatever I said to her worked because, I was invited back to her place for a nightcap (Pussy).

Jade unlocked her door. "Excuse the mess; I'm in the middle of doing laundry."

I walked in. "Its cool ma'. You should see my house on laundry day."

She turned the TV on. "Do you want a drink? I have vodka and Henny."

"I'll take a glass of that Henny."

"Well help yourself; I'm going to go change out of this dress."

I thought to myself (YES! I'm about to get some pussy!) "You need some help in there?" I yelled.

Jade paused for a second, "Umm yea, I could use help unzipping this zipper."

I walked to her bedroom to help unzip the back of her dress. When the dress went down, my dick went up. She had the most amazing skin tone I'd ever seen. I think her breasts were C's or D's and they set straight up. As I took it all this in she slipped on a t-shirt. What the fuck?!? I already seen you naked you can leave that shit off. She probably didn't want to feel like a hoe. Pause! I hate that shit. Why do women try not to have sex on the first day? You know damn well you are going to give the guy some pussy the next time you see him so, why put that shit off? We are both grown here. Let's make with the fucking. Un-Pause.

She must have read my mind because, right after she put on the t-shirt, she jumped in the bed and signaled me to come to her. Needless to say, I put it down (Sex God). After we were done, she laid her head on my chest and leg across my leg. Then she drifted off to dream land. I laid there thinking to myself, "Man, I put her ass to sleep. This bitch fine as hell too. I'm gonna keep this one around." As I'm giving myself props, I felt a warm sensation running down my leg. I was confused. What the fuck could that be? Was she cumming again? Is she a squirter? Nah, that couldn't be what it was. She was sleep. Then it hit me, this bitch is pissing on me!

I jumped up. "Hey girl! What the fuck are you doing? I'm not into that freaky shit. Who do you think you are, the female R. Kelly?"

She woke up confused. "What are you talking about?"

I was all glisteny and shit. "Why are you pissing on me?"

Jade suddenly realized she pissed all over the bed. "I'm so sorry. This is embarrassing. I must have been way too drunk."

"Well damn, I need to take a shower now. You got me all pissy"

She jumped up and ran to the bathroom. "I'll get the water running for you."

I got in the shower and jade followed me. We had sex again in there so; I forgave her for the accidental pissing.

The next day I couldn't get her out of mind. People get drunk and piss themselves all the time so, I let that shit go. Remember, she was a stone cold fox. I called her the next afternoon to invite her to a movie. We hooked up that night for drinks and to watch a chick flick. Everything went fine. It looked like we were in for another night of amazing sex! As we pulled up to her apartment, my penis started to get hard. I don't know why. Maybe mini me had psychic abilities.

Jade jumped out the car. "Let me go straighten up for you real quick."

I was in no rush. "Go for it ma'."

She walked her sexy ass to her apartment as I parked my car. I smoked a cigarette to give her time to get her shit together then, I made my way to her place. I walked in and to my surprise; she was standing in the door way butt ass naked in a pair of red heels. That's what my penis was predicting. Good job mini me. I went Mr. Marcus on her ass. Legs going one way, head going the other way. It went down!

So much so, I needed another cigarette. "I'll be back sexy, I'm gonna walk outside to smoke real quick."

Jade laughed. "I put it on ya huh? I'll be right here waiting for round two."

"Since you put it like that, I'll make this quick."

I looked like a speed walker walking to my car. I unlocked it. I looked for my cigarettes but, I couldn't find them shits anywhere. I looked under my seat, in the center console, and in the backseat. I walked around to the passenger side to see if I may have dropped them over there some kind of way. As I climbed in I felt a cold wet sensation on my hand. What the fuck was that? I used my cell phone light to get a better view. Holy Shit! My seat was soaked all the way through. Did Jade spill a drink in here? Did she even have a drink to spill in here? I bent my head down towards the seat to smell it. [sniff sniff] Yep, it was fucking piss! This bitch done pissed in my fucking car! I said fuck smoking and headed back to Jades apartment to give her a piece of my mind. When I walked in the apartment she was still naked, wearing those sexy ass red heels, and bent over looking for something in the refrigerator. I forgot all about that piss and got in that ass right there in the kitchen. You can say I buttered her biscuits or better yet, fed her some sausage.

After we were done reality hit me. "Hey sexy, I have to go."

Jade stood up. "Why?"

"I got things I gotta do."

She put on her clothes. "Whatever, you just like every other nigga."

"Nah ma'. It's nothing like that. I just gotta go take care of something real quick."

She went off on me. "You know what, fuck you then! Get the fuck out of my house! You not about to treat me like a cheap hoe. What the fuck you got to do, that so damn important, at 3 in the fucking morning?!?"

I thought to myself, I know this girl ain't talking to me like this. I took a deep breath. "Bitch, I gotta go shampoo my fucking car seat! You know, the one you thought was a fucking port-a-potty!"

She shut, what they call, the fuck up when I said that.

I continued to go off. "What kind of girl just goes around pissing in people's cars? All you had to do is ask me to pull over. Fuck this shit; I'm going sleep in a dry bed tonight. I'm out of here!"

I stormed out. Was I mad? Not really. Did I fuck her again? I sure did. I mean, she was a dime to the third power. Hell, I'm actually still fucking her to this day. So what's the moral of the story? The moral of the story is a simple one. Take yo' bitches to the bathroom.

I PRAY THEY SERVE HENNY IN HELL

BEEF WITH THE JAMAICAN MAFIA

At age 21 I was almost killed by the Jamaican Mafia. Nigga what?!? For real? Yes! The shit was crazy. Bullets flying everywhere, bodies dropping like flies, niggas crying and shit. Ok, I might be over exaggerating just a bit. Let me tell you the story and you come to your own conclusion.

It was the summer of 2005. I woke up that morning with every intention of going to work but, somehow I never quite made it. Not because I was lazy, but because I was fucking my supervisor. Let me start from the beginning. After high school I got a pretty decent job. The only downside to this job was that I had to relocate to Mountain Home Idaho. Go ahead, think about where that is for a second. Can you point it out on a map? You can't! I know I couldn't. When they told me this shit I damn near passed out. I was under a binding contract at the time so, I really couldn't back out. So fuck it, I took my ass to Idaho. Gotta get that money right?

Here are a few things you should know about Idaho. First, it's the Arian Nation capital of the world. These are the most racist people on Earth. The KKK ain't got shit on these niggas. Funny story about the Arian Nation though, they beat an old black woman once and she sued them. Not for money but, for their name. She technically owns them now. Ok, where was I? Oh yea, another thing you need to know about Idaho is, there are only about 300 black people living there. What makes this even worse is that 275 of them are men. This means black woman are a high commodity out there.

When I arrived in Idaho, of course, my job sent the only other black person there to come pick me up from the airport. This person just happened to be a black woman and my new supervisor. Her name was. Hold up! I still hope I hit that again. I don't know if I want to put her name out there like that. Oh well fuck it, her name was Briana. She was a sexy little redbone from Montgomery, Alabama. I saw her and thanked my lucky stars, right then and there. Not that it was love at first sight; it was the fact that I would have a black girl to stick my penis in. Pause, I don't have anything against white women. In fact, it's fun to venture off every now and again. I just like a big thick ass and some juicy thighs. Ok, un-pause. We started getting it in that night. I wish I had known what I know now because; maybe things would have been different. By the way, shout out to Briana for not suing me after she reads this.

If I would have went to work that morning, the Jamaican mafia wouldn't have it out for me to this day. Allow me to explain. I woke up late that day. Mainly because, I knew I was fucking my supervisor and I wouldn't get in any trouble. I called into work and of course, Briana let me stay home no questions asked. I smoked "Cigarettes" back then. Not proud of it but hey, everyone's tried it, even Bill Clinton. I was outside smoking in the parking lot of my apartment complex when the shit went down. I was leaning up against this raggedy ass grey Oldsmobile when, I noticed a person in the upstairs window of the apartment across the street making hand gestures at me. I said, "Oh shit, my bad," then waved at the guy in an apologetic manner. I figured I must have been leaning on his car.

I don't think he took my wave as it was intended. I looked up and saw him coming down the stairs of his apartment. He was wearing a bullet proof vest and carrying an AK-47. He screamed with a Jamaican accent, "Get the fuck away from my cars 'mon." How was I supposed to know these were all his cars? I hauled ass to my apartment, grabbed my sawed off and did what any real nigga would have done. I called 911. I was scared out of my fucking mind! I know you might say I bitched out but fuck that shit; I don't wanna be the first nigga to die in Idaho.

The 911 operator said, "911 what's your emergency?"

I screamed. "It's like 50 Jamaicans outside trying to kill me." (It was really just 1 and I actually think he was from the Virgin Islands).

The operator said, "Calm down, where are they now?"

I looked out my window, "Oh shit, this nigga coming across the street." America, this fool, whose name I later found out was Leon, was marching across the street, carrying his riffle, and screaming a cadence. He was acting like he was in the fucking Army or something. I almost shit a brick!

The 911 operator said, "Stay in the house, help is on the way."

I wanted to but, then I started thinking. I'm not just gonna sit in this bitch and wait to die. I'm a man, am I not?!?! I told the operator, "Y'all better hurry up. If this nigga comes in my yard, I'm gonna kill him!" I hung up the phone.

I looked out my blinds to see where he was. He slowed down a bit but was still heading towards my front door. I swung the door open, pointed my gun at him.

"Put your gun down." I don't know why I said that. Like he was gonna say ok, no problem.

He said, "You wanna play a Gangsta' you gotta be a Gangsta', 'mon." Actually, he didn't really say "Mon," I'm just adding that in to give it that Jamaican affect.

"I never said I wanted to be a gangster." I screamed.

He looked at me crazy then, cocked that gun. My heart fell in my stomach. I don't care what any wanna be thug tells you. When you are starring down the barrel of a loaded AK-47, the bitch comes out of you.

I yelled, "Man chill!   I'm sorry! I'm never gonna go by your cars again."

He said, "It's too late to be sorry 'mon."

I thought to myself. I should just shoot this nigga before he shoots me. The thought went through my body then to my trigger finger. I held my breath, tightened my shoulder then, the cops pulled up! Thank God the cops pulled up because, I was about to kill this nigga.

As soon as he seen the lights, he broke out running. This nigga was truly crazy. I think, me leaning on his car was the last straw or something because really, you gonna kill a nigga for leaning on your car? He sprinted back to his apartment. Of course the cops ran after him. I mean, he was a black man, with a gun, in Idaho. I just kind of backed out of the way. This fool barricaded himself in his apartment. He had sandbags and everything. He was ready for war!

After about 2 hours, the cops finally apprehended him. I watched the whole thing go down. After the scene calmed a bit, the cops started questioning people in the complex regarding the incident.

I was asked by an officer, "Did you see what happened?"

I said, "I have no idea what's going on." He moved on to another neighbor.

He asked this older woman, "Did you see what happened. She straight snitched on me. And that's why I don't like old people, always tellin' on people.

The officer came back to me, "I thought you didn't know what was going on?"

My shotgun was then taken and I was arrested on site.

Jail in Idaho sucked. Let me dispel a rumor real quick. I know people say that all black men have big dicks and all white men have little dicks. This is not true! I was waiting on somebody to bail me out when I was moved into the "Holding" cells. This shit looked like Oz on crack! All country fed white boys that didn't like my black ass.

The first night I was there the guard calls out, "Shower time." I didn't move from my cell. He walked over and said, "Did you hear me boy? I said its time to wash your dirty ass."

I said, "Oh its cool, I just got out the shower right before I was arrested. I should be clean enough for about 4 or 5 days."

He yelled, "This is not an option, nigger!"

Ten guys, one shower. Or better yet, nine white guys, one1 black guy, one shower. I was praying please don't let me get raped in here! Then all of a sudden, this 6'6 250lbs white man walked up on me, butt ass naked. He was looking at me like a fat person looks at a Big Mac. I started to think ways I could get him to leave me alone.

He said, "My name is Randy."

I said, "Hi Randy. My name is HIV positive."

Randy Laughed, "You're exotic. Why you in here boy?"

"I was arrested for having sex with women when I knew I had Aids." Of course I didn't really have Aids but, fuck that, I had to do something!

He said, "Oh yea, I got Aids too. We have to stick together."

Then he grabbed his penis. This dude dick looked like a baby's leg. I suddenly felt remorse for all the women of my past that I convinced to have butt sex. I mean honestly, I can barely take a good shit without a little pain. There was no way his dick was gonna fit in my little booty hole.

I said, "Man chill out. Why you rubbing your dick like that?"

Randy said, "I like what I see."

I bellowed, "Fuck that! You ain't bout to rape me!" I karate chopped that bitch in the throat. Then beat the shit out of everybody in the shower. Ok, I'm lying. I screamed like a bitch and called for the guards. Luckily, they came before this dude ever touched me. HE NEVER TOUCHED ME! That's my story and I'm sticking to it! The next day I was charged with brandishing a deadly weapon in public then released on bail. You can Google that shit! Mountain home P.D.

After a short trial, heavy fines, and 6 months probation I was ready to get the fuck out of Idaho. Between the lack of black people, the Jamaican Mafia, and people trying to rape me, I concluded, this was not the living conditions I needed. I packed up and moved to Arizona. So, that's the story of how I almost died by the hands of the Jamaican Mafia. The near death didn't almost come from the stand-off. It almost came as a result of the stand-off, the jail shower.

RAFAEL BECOMES A PIMP: PART I

At age 23 I was a pimp. Not a playa or a guy that got a lot of women (Though, I did get a lot of women). I was really, a true to life, "Bitch, where my money at," Pimp! What?!? How could this be?!? As sad as that may sound, this was my life. I didn't choose this life. It just, kind of fell into my lap one day. I'll start from the beginning and you can be the judge.

Age 23 was my golden year, the year that coincides with the actual date I was born. Not only did it coincide with this date, it was the amount of women I planned to sleep with that year. Wait, I'm getting ahead of myself, that story is actually in a later chapter. And it's fucking epic! Let's get back to this story though. Where was I? Oh yea, it was my golden year. I was recently divorced so, I was out there running wild. I was the king of the strip club! Let me rephrase that. I was the king of going to the strip club already drunk and not ordering shit. I never made it rain nor did I participate in many lap dances. I figured I could watch good basketball games and see some titties while I was there. That's what we call a win-win. Anyway, the strip club became my second home. Pause, anyone you see in a strip club on a regular bases, has had sex with at least one stripper there. So ladies, if your dude is in the strip club once a month. He's probably, at a minimum, fucking one of the waitresses. Sorry fellas, that was relevant to my story. Un-Pause.

I was in the strip club at least once a month. So following my own logic, I must have been fucking a stripper right? Nope! Ain't that sum shit? All the money I considered and almost spent on potential or possible future lap dances, and I get no love? Maybe it's because I wasn't making it rain every night but, I don't think the strippers saw me in their future. That's until one summer night. A new girl walked in. She was covered up but, I could tell by her face she was a dime. She rushed off to the back to change. When she came out, every nigga in that bitch went crazy! Including me! After her stage performance, instead of picking money up like a traditional stripper would, she just walked off the stage. Security came out with Winn-Dixie bags and collected the money for her. That's how bad she was!

Later that night she passed by me on her way to the bar. I grabbed her gently to get her attention and a dance from this big fine motha fucka.

"Hey sexy, let me buy you a drink. What do you want?"

She replied, "A bottle of Grey Goose."

I paused for a second, gathered my thoughts, then said, "I'm sorry, what do you want to drink?"

"A bottle of Grey Goose, nigga you deaf?"

She wanted a whole damn bottle of Grey Goose! Bitch must have lost her fucking mind. Do you know what a woman has to do for me to buy them an entire bottle of liquor? I'm going to need a kidney or something. And this wasn't even fucking cheap liquor from Wal-Mart. This was the club. Club prices are usually $300 dollars a bottle!

I let her hand go, "I don't have Grey Goose money but, I can get you a shot and a nice tip after a lap dance.

She sighed in disgust, "I guess."

We took our shot then went to the lap dance area. She went to work on me. But this trick had game America! As she danced on, me she ordered shot after shot of Grey Goose. I was already drunk so, these back to back shots were fucking me up.

About four songs later she got off me, "That's 200."

"200 dollars!?!"

She placed her hand on her hip, "Yea, plus your tab at the bar is like, 150. You can give me mines in cash though."

"Girl you crazy." I said.

She started snapping and jerking her neck like all ghetto women do, "Nigga fo' songs, 50 dollars a dance, equals 200; add it up."

I started to add it up. And wouldn't you know it, this bitch was right. I owed this girl 200 dollars for dancing. I mean, she didn't suck my dick or nothing.

"Damn I guess you right. Let me pay for this liquor first then I'll hit the ATM and give you your cash. I don't have 200 dollars on me right now.

"Ok, I'll be waiting right here." She said.

I went to the bar to settle my tab. The bartender looked up at me, "That'll be 300 dollars."

"What?!? The dancer just told me $150." I shouted.

He looked at security and signaled them over. "She told you wrong nigga, you owe me $300."

Now, he wasn't about to just punk me out of my money. Hell, I could have got a bottle if I was paying that much. I said, "Explain to me how the fuck I owe you 300 dollars before I set it off in this bitch." Nah, I'm joking I didn't really say that. What I really said was, "How do I owe so much? Aren't shots only 10 dollars? I only had about 5."

"You had six and your dancer had eight. House liquor is 10 a shot but, y'all were drinking that Goose so that's 20 a shot. Plus my $20 dollar tip for keeping them coming adds up to 300 mother fucking dollars."

I thought about it for a second. The nigga was absolutely right so I paid. After I paid him the stripper was right up in my face.

"Now let's walk to this ATM so I can get what's mine."

"Look ma, we gonna have to work something out. I don't have that much money." I pointed to the bartender. "That nigga just charged me 300 dollars for your drinks."

The stripper rolled her eyes, "Look baby, I'm sorry to have to play you like this but, this is how it's done here. We dance on drunk niggas. They forget the prices then, we run up their tab."

"Well I'll be damned. Y'all scamming niggas in here." I said.

"Look this was my first night so, that's why I went so hard on you." Then she said, "Give me 60 dollars to cover my house fee and fill my tank up with your credit card or something and we can call it even."

I said, "Cool." Then gave her exactly 60 dollars and followed her to the gas station.

She pulled up to the pump and rolled her window down. "You could drove off. Why didn't you?"

"I'm a man of my word." Honestly, I was so drunk, I didn't even think about it. Oh well fuck it.

"My name is Lorana, by the way."

I thought for a second. Lorana? Like the chick that chopped ol' boy dick off? Then I said, "I'm Brandon." This was the name I gave to women I had no intention of being with long-term.

Lorana smiled, "You seem like a nice guy. Do you wanna grab a bite to eat?"

Now, do you remember at the beginning of the story when I described her? She looked fucking amazing! Unfortunately, I had to pass. I shook my head, "I would but, it's already close to midnight and I have to be at work in the morning.

Lorana said, "I understand. Do you wanna trade numbers? Maybe we can hook up later."

I pulled my phone out so fast I gave my hand a rug burn off the denim in my pocket. We traded numbers then, I went home.

The next day she hit me up around 6pm. I answered the phone, "Hello."

Lorana's voice was so sexy. "Hey Brandon, this is Lorana. Are you coming to the club tonight? I want to see you."

"Nah, I'm hurting from last night I'm just gonna chill to the house. Maybe this weekend I might swang through."

She sounded disappointed, "Well, can I come kick it with you? I'll bring a bottle."

How do you say Cha-Ching in stripper language?!! YES, Booty Call!!!! I'd never fucked a stripper before but, I have heard it was amazing so I immediately said, "Sure what time?"

"Is 8 or 9 ok?"

"Yea I'll probably be chilling by the hot tub BBQn."

I don't know why I said this. I mean my apartment complex did have a hot tub but, she already knew I was broke from the night before so, why play like I was a baller? Anyway she said, "Cool text me the directions."

We hung up and I sprung into action. No time to wash and dry my sheets so I Febreezed the fuck out of them, cleaned my shower real quick, washed my dishes, took some meat out to BBQ by the hot tub, then vacuumed my living room. Pause. Women; men only clean when there is an imminent chance of us having sex. Un-Pause. After about an hour, I had the apartment in tip top shape. Next, I fired up the BBQ pit and cracked open a bottle of mascato. Before I knew I heard a knock on the door.

"Come in."

Lorana walked in and I swear everything went into slow motion. She looked like a mix between Megan Good, Lauren London, and Pinky (porn star). My dick got hard immediately. She was wearing a red G string bikini with a white wrap and of course, glass heels.

She gave me a hug, "Well damn, someone's happy to see me."

Yes, she was talking about my dick. That shit kept rising like the gas price. I just chuckled then went to close the door.

She said, "Wait my home girl coming."

"Home girl?"

"Yeah, I told her where I was going tonight and she asked if she could come. I hope that's cool."

I said, "Sure pretty lady, no sweat."

I might have spoken those words but, what I really meant was, I don't want another one of your stripper friends in my fucking house. I don't know y'all bitches like that. But then, she walked in. DAMN!!!! She was badder than Lorana.

"Hi, you must be Brandon. I'm Lorana's roommate, Maria."

Oh yes, she was a Puerto Rican goddess. I looked her up and down. "Nice to meet you."

Lorana said, "Do you have a roommate or do you live alone?"

"I live alone but, my homeboy stays right around the corner."

She ask me to hit him up so he can keep my girl company. I sent him a text asap. We went out by the hot tub and BBQ'ed. It started to get late and my home boy still hadn't hit me back so, I sent him another text. He texted back, "I'm good I'm chillin with my lil chick tonight." I tried to explain how fine this bitch was but, he wasn't comprehending so, I moved on to plan B. I texted every dude in my phone a picture of these two chicks eating BBQ, by the hot tub, in skimpy ass bikinis. Do you know how many niggas hit me back? None! These niggas have all been cut from my circle since then. Anyway, I was down to the bare minimum.

Maria looked like she was getting tired of seeing Lorana hugging on me and said, "Girl that food was good. Are we still going to pass by the club for a quick drink though?"

In other words, I'm bored, you're my ride, and I'm ready to go when you are. I picked up on this and went into the apartment. I grabbed a list of co-worker's phone numbers I kept in my kitchen drawer incase I ever had a work emergency. I texted all the guys on there I thought might be cool, outside of work, the picture of the girls with this message attached: "I have two freaky, and drunk strippers ready to get loose, who is going to help me? If you come just remember my name is Brandon."

This guy we called Dash hit me back in .056 seconds. I lived right around the corner from the guy. He got there in less than 5 minutes. I introduced him to the ladies. This seemed to be working out. Maybe I should have been hanging out with Dash. He had Maria all cuddled up on the side of the hot tub so, that left me time to start fondling Lorana.

I said, "It's starting to get a bit chilly out here. Y'all wanna head to the apartment?" Everyone agreed because, everyone knew it was time to do some fucking!

As soon as we got to the apartment the girls asked if they could take a shower to rinse the chlorine out of their hair. I said sure and they stripped right there. Oh yea, I totally forgot these weren't regular girls they were strippers so, they are use to being naked. They showered together and left the door open. It was turning out to be the best night of my life! When they came out of the shower, they asked for T-Shirts. I gave them both one. Then we started taking shots. For the next hour we listen to music, drunk liquor, and grinded on each other. We were all good and wasted when Maria went to the bathroom.

She walked out with a sexy smile on her face. "Brandon, thanks for letting me hangout with you guys today and for introducing me to Dash."

"No problem ma'."

She looked at Dash. "You're pretty cool Dash, I enjoyed hanging out with you."

Dash smiled, "Your pretty cool too Ms. Maria."

Maria yawned, "It's getting late. I need to get in my bed."

Pause . Before I tell you the next part. Keep in mind Dash and Maria had been grinding on each other for the past 2-3 hours. Ok, un-pause.

Dash said, "Yeah it is getting late." He stood up, gave her a hug, dapped me up, waved bye to Lorana and said, "I'll get up with yall." Then he dashed clean out the door.

Maria looked at Lorana. "What the fuck was that?"

Lorana shrugged her shoulders. "I don't know girl."

Maria said, "Brandon, what the fuck is up with your homeboy?"

I was confused my damn self. "I don't think he caught the signs."

Maria was pissed. "Well damn, they were as clear as day. I told you bye then told him I was ready to get in bed. What the fuck he wanted me to do? Pull his dick out and say stick it in me?"

I chuckled, "I can call him back. I'm sure he's not too far yet.

Maria said, "Nah that dude was kinda lame anyway. I just haven't been fucked in a while. Lorana, can you bring me home please?"

Lorana stood up, "Yeah girl. Just let me get dressed."

I almost cried. "Nah for real, let me call him back."

They just kind of shook their heads and headed towards the door. Man I was pissed. Fucking Dash! This is why I don't hang out with work niggas. They left me sitting on a couch in my boxers, drunk as hell, and horny as fuck.

I texted dash and went off on him. He texted me back, "My Bad." My bad?!? This dude fucked my pussy up, and all he can say is my, fucking, bad. I cooled down a bit then curled up on the couch. I replayed the night over and over in my head. The opportunity to have sex with the hottest women I'd ever seen in my life had just slipped though my finger tips. I heard a knock on the door. This must be Dash coming to either apologize or fight. I mean, the text message I sent was pretty harsh.

Still pissed, I screamed, "Come in!" To my surprise, it was Lorana and Maria. "Y'all alright?" I asked.

Lorana said, "Yea we just went to the gas station up the street."

Maria reached into her purse and pulled out a box of condoms (Extra Large), looked at them for a second, then tossed them to me. "It's your lucky night; I hope you can handle two freaks."

Can you say Ear to Ear Smile?! For the Next hour I did everything I always seen in porno movies. I had one pussy on my face, one on my crotch. I'm going to stop right there because they might censor my book if I go too deep into details. To better paint the picture, do this. Go to a popular black porn website. Click on the featured video. Then imagine my face on the dude plowing the women in the scene. That's how serious this was!

Wait, Put this book down first. I don't want the pages to get all sticky. This seems like a good place to take a break. So I'll let you stand up and stretch out, grab a soda, and I'll continue in the a few. You're probably saying, "Where the hell is the story about being a PIMP?!" I'm going to get to that.

This is a long ass story so I had to split this bitch into two chapters. Be patient, it's coming my friend. Oh yea, shout out to Dash. I hope you read this and remember you almost cost me sex with a dime. Luckily, my swag saved me and I turned that into my first threesome! So, I guess I owe you a bunch. Thanks homie!

To Be Continued...

RAFAEL BECOMES A PIMP: PART II

At age 23 I was a pimp. Yep, I was a real life, "Where my hoes at," pimp. If you skipped the last chapter, allow me to recap the events that led up to this story then, I'll continue and let you be the judge.

I met a stripper named Lorana. I thought she was the most amazing looking woman I'd ever seen in my life, until I met her roommate, Maria. I invited them to my apartment for a poolside BBQ, drinks, and music. They insisted that I call a male friend over to keep Maria company so, I called a dude I worked with named Dash. Dash agreed to come over and help me entertain the women. The night was looking very promising. And when I say promising, I mean it looked like we were about to fuck! After a while in the hot tub, we retired to the apartment for some privacy and some obvious fucking. Maria seemed to be interested in Dash. She displayed all the signs and even gave him an invite to her bed. Well, this simple mother fucker missed all that shit and went home, leaving me alone with two horny strippers. The strippers were pissed! After Dash left they cracked a few jokes about how lame he was then decided to go home. Ain't this some Shit! Dash just single handedly ruined my chances to fuck the baddest chick I'd ever met. After everyone left, I curled up on my couch confused, horny, and pissed off. Then all of a sudden, I heard a knock at the door. It was Lorana and Maria! Maria pulled out a box of condoms and said, "It's your lucky night, I hope you can handle two freaks." Hard to believe? Well, believe it! That shit happened. I got it on tape! Anyway, that's where this chapter picks up.

The threesomes continued for the next few weeks. Lorana was, what I guess you can call, my girlfriend so, our sex life was pretty regular. Maria only joined us about once a week but, when she did it was fucking awesome! Lorana and I spent a lot of time together. We became inseparable. I was starting to fall in love with the girl. Yes, I was in love with a stripper (T. Pain voice). She was a freak too. She let me do just about anything I wanted in the bedroom. One time, I skeeted on her face. The next day she had a pimple on her forehead. All I could think was "Damn, I got her face pregnant." Irrelevant, I know. But it's hilarious. Just when everything was going good, the inevitable problems arose. No, I wasn't tripping on her shaking her ass for niggas in the club. Hell, I was in there as much as her! Her problem was money. She hit a few financial snags. I found out one evening over dinner.

She looked up at me like a sad puppy. "Brandon." Pause! Just in case you forgot from the last chapter this girl thought my name was Brandon, the name I give one night stands. Un-Pause.

"Brandon, Maria is having trouble coming up with her half of the rent. Do you have any money I can get to help us out?"

"Sorry sexy. I wish I did but, I'm barely making ends meet." Of course I had a couple grand in my savings but, this broad wasn't getting none of that. Money over bitches, remember. Ok, I didn't have shit in my savings and I probably would have given it to her if I did. I told you, I was in love with this chick. Lorana was evicted a few weeks later. When she told me, she had that "my dog just died" look on her face.

I said, "Man that sucks. What are you going to do?"

"Well I was hoping I could stay with you for a few days until I can find another place."

I didn't know what to say. I didn't want a stripper living with me. I mean the sex was cool but, the day to day headache may not be worth it. Despite my strong want NOT to have her stay with me, I said, "Sure sexy, you can stay with me but, only for about a week. My lease has strong rules on the number of occupants." Hopefully, she caught on to what I was saying, I DON'T WANT YOU HERE!

Well America, she sure didn't catch on to my underlined message. Lesson learned, next time just be straight forward. The one week limit I gave her turned into about three. Then, get this shit, she asked if Maria could stay too. But look how they tried to they played me. Pause. Looking back on this story, I realize I'm not looking like much of a "G" right now but, these bitches were bad so, I'm sure any fella out there would have done the same thing. Un-Pause. Lorana and I were gearing up for another amazing night of fucking when, she asked, "Do you mind if Maria joins us tonight."

"Of course I don't."

"I knew you wouldn't, she's meeting me to the store. Im gonna grab a bottle of Henny so we can do it big. Do you need anything?"

I smirked, "Grab a box of extra large condoms and a pack of Newport's."

Lorana Chuckled, "You sure you want extra large?"

"Girl don't play with me." I said with a Smile. "You know what I'm working with."

She laughed again, "I know exactly what you working with. That's why I asked hahahaha."

I started to go in on her but, I just laughed and handed her 5 bucks for my smokes. Lorana left and retuned with Maria in no time.

She walked through the door then kissed me on my cheek, "They were out of Newports baby. I got you Kools instead."

Maria grinned, "And we got you that pack of extra 'smedium condoms you asked for."

I grabbed the bag with a smile, "Shut up. Did y'all get the Henny?"

Lorana walked towards the door, "Oops, forgot to get it. I'll be right back."

Maria headed over to hug me as Lorana walked out the door. "I've missed you." Then she grabbed my dick. "And I missed him. Let's do it before Lorana gets back."

I laughed and attempted to play it off like she was joking. This was out of character for Maria. Normally, when she would join Lorana and I for sex, she would be more reserved until we were under the covers. It's not that I didn't want to fuck Maria right then and there, it's just that I needed that liquor in my system if I planned on lasting longer than ten minutes. I put on some music and offered her a glass of wine to kill time. Lorana took damn near forever. She finally came back. She walked in the apartment. The first thing she saw was Maria sitting on my lap, Cowgirl style. I thought she might trip but, she just poured us shots and asked if we wanted to play a drinking game. I quickly responded, "Yes."

Lorana pulled out a deck of cards. "We'll keep it simple. We'll draw cards. Whoever has the lowest car has to take a shot."

I looked at Maria. "I'm down. That sounds easy enough."

The game began and quickly ended. This was a fucking setup. These bitches must be professional blackjack dealers or something because; I kept getting the low card. I took about 7 shots in 10 minutes. Trust me, don't play this game. It's fucking cruel. After the game ended, they were all over each other. I watched for a second then, maneuvered my way in the middle of them. Somehow, I ended up hitting Maria from the back while Lorana was under us, licking my balls and eating Maria's pussy.

As I was drilling the shit out of Maria, she turned her head back and looked me in the eyes. "Put it in my ass."

Well you know what I did, I stuck that dick dead in her booty. She moaned sounds of pleasure.

Lorana, still licking my balls, said, "That sounds like it feels good. My turn."

I looked down at her. "Alright let me change the condom."

As I pulled my dick out to change the condom, Maria's body locked up. You want believe what happen next. SHE SHIT ALL OVER LORANA!!!! Fucking gross!

Lorana jumped up, "Oh my god, what the fuck did you do?"

Maria started crying. "I so sorry. I didn't mean too. I was trying to hold it but, he went to deep." (who got a smedium dick now?)

Lorana started walking to the bathroom, I yelled. "Don't move. Your dripping shit all over my carpet. Let me get you a towel."

I handed her a towel then she wiped up. They showered and cleaned my living room from top to bottom. I was pissed off the whole time they cleaning. I took more shots then went to bed. They joined me a few minutes later. Get this! They were still trying to have sex. I thought about it for a second then, went with it. I mean, they were clean now. Plus, a little shit never hurt nobody.

The next morning I woke up to two beautiful women, topless, cooking breakfast for me. I walked in the kitchen. "This is the life."

Lorana handed me a plate of food. "Can Maria stay with us for a few days? We move into our place in two weeks."

Us?!? What the fuck did she mean us? Bitch, you don't stay here, I do. Of course I didn't say that. I said, "Sure but, just a few days." The arrangement turned out to be AMAZING! I was living every single man's dream. Two dimes, walking around, butt ass naked, cooking for me, rubbing my back and shit. I thought I had died and gone to heaven!

One night Lorana asked me, "Can you drive me to this bachelor party I'm doing? My car is acting up. "

"Sure, where is it?"

"Scottsdale."

"Damn, that's where the ballas at. Aight I'll bring you. How you gonna get back?"

"Can you pick me up too please?"

"Damn, I don't have gas for all that. What time?"

Lorana smiled, "Don't worry about the gas baby, I got you. I have to be there soon. I'll be done by 10pm."

"Well let's bust a move then sexy."

I dropped her off to this little mini mansion in Scottsdale, and then I hung out at the local sports bar until she called me to pick her up. It didn't take as long as I thought. When I arrived to pick her up, she was already standing outside.

Lorana got in the car. "Thanks baby. Here's your gas money."

She handed me over 200 dollars. I gave her a surprised look. "200 dollars for gas?"

"Yes, thanks for helping me and my girl out these last few weeks. "

This exact routine went on for the next two weeks with her and Maria. I would bring them to bachelor's parties and when I would pick them up, they would give me about 200 dollars. This had me thinking about shaking my ass for money. I started to get use to all of that fast cash. This was until one night I was picking Maria up from a party.

She got in the car. "Sorry, I can't give you any gas money."

"It's cool, you gave me more than enough."

Maria kissed me on the cheek. "I mean, I would but that joker didn't pay me. You think you can ask him for my money?"

I was furious. "Why didn't he pay you?"

"He said I didn't do enough."

"Let me go talk to him."

I got out the car and rung the door bell. The door swung open. A guy in a robe was standing there.

He looked me up and down. "What do you want?"

I replied, "Can you pay the girl for dancing?"

"Who are you her Pimp? That bitch didn't even wanna suck my dick."

Maria screamed from the car, "I told you that was extra!"

I was confused as fuck. Hold the fuck up. What kind of bachelor party was this? Where the fuck was all the other people at?

I pulled myself together. "Look man, it's not that type of party. Just pay the girl for her dance and we'll be out of your hair."

The man looked at me then reached into his desk drawer. Is he pulling out a gun? My heart fell in my stomach. Thank God it was a bill fold instead.

He handed me 400 dollars. "Here, now get off my property before I call the cops. And FYI, your little tramp's pussy wasn't as good as I heard, that's false advertisement."

I walked back to my car. As I started to drive off, I handed Maria the money. "Do you want to explain what that nigga was talking about?"

Maria sighed, "We been sleeping with men for money so we can get this condo next month."

I slammed on the brakes. "What! Y'all got me tied up in some illegal shit. Bitch, I got a good job I can't be fucking around with ya'll."

Lorana backed up in her seat. "I'm sorry. I thought you knew. Who gives 200 dollars for gas money? That was your cut for helping us. The client would see you pull up and then they would pay us. This was the only way we could make sure we didn't get fucked over."

"So y'all some fucking prostitutes?"

The drive home was long and quiet. When we got home, I told them that they had two days to gather their things and get out my house. I was having a good time and making more money than ever but, I couldn't risk my job over this bullshit. Well America, that's the story of how I became a pimp at age 23.

The next day I went to work. I felt bad for snapping on the girls. Then I felt fucking stupid. I had money, pussy, and bitches doing just about anything I wanted them to. I said fuck it. If I'm meant to be a pimp then I meant to be a pimp. I rushed home from work to tell the girls they could stay as long as they wanted. When I opened my apartment door, that shit was empty! I backed up to check the apartment number. I must have gone in the wrong door. This could not be my apartment? I walked in and it sure was my place. I could still see the shit stains on the carpet that Lorana tried every day to clean up. These bitches had robbed me blind. The moral of the story is, don't trust stripper bitches. Oh, and despite me being robbed, let's not overlook the fact that I had more threesomes over the last month than any man you know will have in his lifetime! I'm fucking WINNING!

THE CRYING GAME

At the Age 25, I had sex with 25 women in one year. What?!?   Blew you out the water just now! You probably don't know whether to applaud me or quarantine me. I know, kind of farfetched.   But, I am a direct descendent of Wilt Chamberlin. Ok, I'm bullshitting.   And, I didn't really have that much sex. But, I damn sure tried! Let me start from the beginning and let you be the judge.

In 2009 I found out my employer had plans to relocate half my work division to Germany for exactly one year. Our goal was to integrate with these European motherfuckers, trading ideas and business techniques. Pause! I know I haven't explained what my job is in this entire book but, if I could I would. Too bad that shit is G-14 classified. Let's get this shit straight though, I'm not a drug dealer and I'm not a male prostitute (Though that would be fun). Un-Pause... The news about the move couldn't have come at a worse time. I was two seconds away from proposing to my girlfriend and one second from getting out of the game for good. When I say the game I mean fucking bitches, of course.

Before I left America, my girl and I agreed not to let the year of separation kill our relationship. Anyone that has ever been in a long distance relationship knows this promise never last longer than a month. Well, for me, this shit didn't last the 14 hour flight to Europe. Seven hours into the flight I was balls deep in my first European pussy ever. I didn't even say a word. I just gave that look, felt that vibe, and waited for the invite to the bathroom. Boo-yaahh! Instant member of the Mile High Club! That's when it hit me, I have serious issues. I'm pretty much a dog in expensive sheep's clothing. If I wanted to marry my girl back in America, I had to get all this fucking out of my system. I had to overload the nympho inside me, with sex. I discussed this theory with one of my fellow co-workers. He was half sleep so, I just continued to ponder ways I could accomplish this.

We finally made it to Germany. The group consists of six team members. First there was Mark. He was a pretty laid back guy. I worked with him before but, never directly on a project. Next, was Jeremy. He was from somewhere up north and thought he was better than me in everything but, I think he was gay (never confirmed that). Then there was me, who you all know and love. Yeah there were three other people but, they were all douches so I never really spoke to them.

As we checked into our hotels, I told mark and Jeremy about my sex addiction. "Man this is my last year fucking random bitches. I'm getting married when I get back we get back to the States."

Mark looked at me crazy. "What the fuck are you talking about?"

Jeremy jumped in before I could answer. "Man, he was talking this gay shit on the plane."

"It's not gay. I'm getting old." I replied.

Mark shook his head. "I don't know. It sounds real homo to me."

"Fuck both of y'all. I'm gonna fuck a shit load of bitches this year and get that shit out my system once and for all."

Jeremy laughed. "You mean you're gonna watch a shit load of porn and jack off a few times a day."

"Nigga please. I already smashed a lil German chick on the flight over here. I get pussy son"

"Bullshit, you're lying," Mark said.

"I haven't lied on my dick since '99. Smell my fingers."

"I'm a grown ass man. I'm not smelling yo' fuckin' fingers. Probably smells like old tuna anyway."

Jeremy said, "I bet I can get more pussy out here than you, Rafael."

"No you can't. I do this for a living. To me, getting pussy is an art."

Jeremy chuckled. "I bet I can fuck 2 girls a month until we leave here."

"What 24 women in a year?" I asked.

"Yes"

"Man that ain't shit. If you fuck 24 then, I'll get 25. And I put money on that."

"How much? Put a grand on it."

"That's chump change. I got two."

Jeremy extended his hand to shake mine. "That's a bet."

"Well, I'm already up one so I suggest you get started."

Jeremy shook his head no. "No, it's from this point on. Only on German soil."

Mark, who was watching and cracking up laughing, said, "Y'all dudes wild. This should be an interesting year."

I looked at mark. "You damn right its gonna be interesting. Especially if I don't have my 2 G's when reach 25."

We all checked into our hotel rooms. I forgot all about the bet until about two o'clock that night, someone knocked on my door. I said "Who is it." A voice said, "It's one to zero, that's who it is." I'll be got damned, it was Jeremy.

I opened the door. "What do you mean it's one to zero?"

"I mean, I just got number 1 and you are still on zero."

"How'd you get number one already?"

Jeremy smirked. "Skill homie. The little chick at the receptionist desk came by my room when she finished her shift."

"Damn, I was gonna holla at her tomorrow. Man, whatever. I'm going back to bed"

"Aight goodnight you ol' in second place ass nigga."

"Fuck you."

I slammed the door and went to sleep. I was just blowing smoke about this damn bet but, looks like I might have to come up with 2 grand when I leave here. I thought about it for a second. Wait a minute, I'm a fucking Sex God! I can get any chick I want! Let the Race begin!!!!!

The next few months Jeremy and I went head to head. We talked about the women as if they were statistics, never saying their names only what number they were on our list. It started to get out of hand. Pause. Here's a little known fact. European women love black men! Un-Pause. Americans in the area were limited to a few night clubs so, before we knew it, we couldn't go anywhere without bumping into one of our numbers. I remember walking into a popular club called Rave. As soon as we walked in a chick hugs me and kisses me on my cheek. Then she looks and Jeremy in amazement, and kisses him as well. We walk away and head to a table.

Jeremy chuckled. "You know you pretty much just had my dick on your cheek.

"What the fuck you talking about?"

Jeremy smiled. "That girl at the door was number 11. Got it last night homie."

I laughed. "Well in that case, when you fucked her you basically sucked my dick."

Jeremy's face looked perplexed. "Nigga please. You didn't hit that."

I pulled my phone out my pocket. "Then why did she send me this naked picture? That's number seven for me bruh. How my dick taste?"

Jeremy sighed. "She brushed her teeth so fuck. Let's order some drinks."

We took shot after shot of Henny and tried to talk to almost every nice looking girl there. It looked like we may have drunk this well dry. We ended up drinking with two pretty cool but, obviously gay chicks. I mean they weren't the pretty lesbians we all love. These were the Butch kind with corn rolls and tight sports bras to flatten their titties. Not cute at all. Jeremy got up to go to the bathroom.

When he left the chick-dudes asked me, "You wanna smoke a cigarette with us? We about to step outside real quick."

"Yeah I'll smoke with y'all just let me finish this drink."

The chick-dudes stood up and started walking towards to the door. "Aight we'll be out there behind the building."

I took my time finishing my drink so that I could tell Jeremy that I was going outside to smoke but, he must have been taking a shit or something because, he was taking forever. I finished my drink and headed behind the building to smoke. When I got out there the two chick-dudes where going at it. I mean hands down each other's pants, one leg cocked up on a trashcan. It was the most disturbing thing I'd ever saw yet, I couldn't look away. They noticed I was there and caught me staring. They didn't mind me one bit so, I tried to see if I could get a little action. They might have been chick-dudes but, they still had pussies!

As I got closer the chick-dudes stopped kissing. "What do you think you're doing?"

"I thought y'all might need some dick up in here somewhere."

They laughed. "We straight pretty boy."

"Y'all sure? I'll fuck the shit out y'all"

They looked at each other for a second. "You know what fuck it. On one condition though."

"What's that?"

"You have to let one of us stick a finger in your booty."

I looked at the ground and shrugged my shoulders. "Fuck it. Let's go."

They laughed. "Oh shit! I can't believe you said yes. Let's get it then. You got a condom?"

"Hold that thought."

I didn't have any protection so I sprinted back into the club to see if Jeremy had some. When I got there he was closing the bar tab.

"Man, where the hell you been? And where them bitches go? I'm not paying this whole tab by myself."

"Look Bruh, don't worry about the tab I got that shit. Nigga, I need a condom. ASAP!"

"A condom... For what?

"Because I got 11 and 12, ready to go, in behind the ally, behind the building, right now."

Jeremy smirked. "Nigga you lying. You can't be making up bitches just because you losing."

"I'm not lying homie. The two Dike chicks ready to get down. The only catch is, I gotta let one of 'em stick their finger in my ass."

Jeremy took a step back. "Eww nigga, that's gay."

"That's not gay. Every man has to go to the doctor, at one point, and get that shit done to them for free. At least this way, I get to get some pussy out the deal."

Jeremy shook his head. "As a friend I'm not giving you the condoms Raph. You're drunk and you're not thinking straight."

"Nigga if you don't, I'm gonna raw dog them hoes so, you can save my life or my booty hole. One of the two."

Jeremy reached into his pocket. "Man, here. Take the damn condom. I'm going home. This too much gayness in here for me."

I sprinted to the back of the building and wore them chick-dudes out! Pause. Nobody stuck a finger in my booty. I wouldn't go out like that. That's my story and I'm sticking to it. Un-Pause. We left from behind the club and went our separate ways. I went back in the club to see if Jeremy was still there and to get another drink. That's when I met her. Candace A.K.A. Number 13! The chemistry was there and we headed back to my hotel. Hold up! Did you see what just happened there? Three bitches in one night. Granted two of them acted like dudes but, bitches all the same. I think that's a fucking world record or something. Anyway, back to the story.

I took Candace back to my hotel for a nightcap (sex). We had a few cocktails while she told me about herself. Man this chick was the shit! She was a little sexy redbone. She was mixed, French and African America. She had the sexiest accent ever! Plus she loved football and we had the same favorite movie. This chick was too cool. Can you fall in love in one night? I was starting to feel bad that I would have to make her another number on my list. Oh well fuck it, I have a fucking bet to win.

I sat next to Candace. "Are you spending the night with me?"

Candace stood up. "Well yea, it's three o'clock in the morning. But, I gotta let you know. We are not having sex. I don't get down like that on the first night."

I've heard that shit a thousand times. So, I smiled. "Ok sexy. I won't do anything you don't want me to do."

I put on some music then, we cuddled for the next hour. This bitch wouldn't budge. I kept trying to get it. She wouldn't even come out of her shirt. After a while I could tell she was getting frustrated so I quit trying. I mean, I didn't wanna look like a douche. My dick, however, wasn't on the same page with my thoughts. That shit was rock fucking solid!

She felt it digging in her spine. "Look, we aren't having sex tonight. I think I should go."

"My bad ma', my dick just won't go down."

She laughed. "I can see. It's partly my fault. Let me help you out."

Candace unzipped my pants and gave me the best blow job I ever had! I mean, my toes were curling up and everything! She left shortly after. I immediately called Jeremy to brag about my crazy night. Of course he hated on me and said the chick dudes didn't count. Plus, he claimed head was not sex so, I was still losing. I went to bed a few minutes later.

The next day all I could think about was Candace. She was probably the coolest woman I'd ever met. Plus that head was amazing! Was I sprung? I stopped talking to almost every chick in my phone. Candace and I spent the next few days getting to know each other but, no sex yet. I liked her and all but, the no sex thing was driving me crazy. I was going to have to break it off with her. I broke the news to her one night over dinner.

"Candace, you're a pretty cool chick but, I'm a sex addict so, I kinda need to know if we are going to have sex soon. If not, I can't promise that I won't have sex with another chick. "

Candace sighed. "Rafael, I want nothing more than to have sex with you. I'll come over tonight."

I smiled. "I'm not trying to pressure you."

Candace laughed. "No, I want too."

Later that night Candace came over to my hotel room. She walked in the room and we went at it like animals. We were kissing like we haven't seen each other in years. I threw her on the bed. She turned the lamp off and started to give me some of that amazing head. I raised her dress up. Fuck a condom, I'm going in for the kill before she changes her mind. Pause. Shit about to get crucial. Un-Pause!

I threw up! Why did I throw up? Because this bitch wasn't a bitch! She, was a fucking he! A fucking Shim (she + him).

"BITCH YOU A MAN?!?!?!?!?"

Candace stood up. "I tried to tell you."

"Fuck that nigga. I'm about to whip your monkey ass."

He/She started screaming. "Help! Help!"

I said, "Calm down! Get the fuck out of my room!"

Candace grabbed her/his things. "I thought we had a lot in common."

"Yea a whole lot, starting with, A FUCKING DICK!"

That nigga left my hotel room and I left Europe the next day. I was traumatized. I never paid Jeremy the money for quitting the bet. But fuck him, if he knew what I been through, he would have paid me for losing. Do I feel gay? Fuck no, I was bamboozled (Malcolm X Voice). Am I the number one suspect in the death of a German cross dresser? Who Knows?!?!? (No body, no murder). So what's the moral of the story? The moral is a simple one. If her hair is flawless, she looks like she's never been bit by a mosquito, if her head game is un-humanly amazing, and she likes all the same shit that you like then, she's probably a man! For now on, I grab a woman's crotch before I kiss her. I'd rather get a sexual assault charge than get head from another SHIM!

RAFAEL RECEIVES RAPTURE

"Be watchful, and strengthen the things which remain, that are ready to die: for I have not found thy works perfect before God. Remember therefore how thou hast received and heard, and hold fast, and repent. If therefore thou shalt not watch, I will come on thee as a thief, and thou shalt not know what hour I will come upon thee." **- Jesus Christ**

At age 32 I received rapture. Wait, what?!? Yep, the end of the world came. Don't ask me how or why, the shit just happened. Alright, let me start from the beginning. It was a late and peaceful night. I had just finished praying. Ok, I'm lying I was actually sleeping off a hangover. I went to this crazy ass bachelor party the night before and got shit faced. It started out with private strippers. The private strippers led to body shots, body shots led to a roof top party and then somehow, a goat ended up on doing a keg stand. We recorded it. That shit ended up on YouTube. It was bananas! But anyway, I was sleeping off a hangover.

I was awakened to the vision of my mother holding me in her arms. I felt as if I was a newborn infant. It was my first memory, I think. I sort of drifted away from that memory like a feather caught in a gentle stream of air when, all of a sudden; I was reliving the memory of my father teaching me to ride a bike. In the blink of an eye I was reliving my first fight. Then, losing my virginity. It was now clear; I was reliving all the high points in my life. This all took place as I was drifting towards a glow that resembled the Northern Lights. At first I thought it was a trippy ass dream but, somehow, I was floating away from my body. I started to panic, trying to get back to my body but, it wasn't working. I was still floating up. I figured I must have died so I stopped trying to fight it.

As I floated towards this bright ass light somewhere in outer space, I realized I wasn't the only one. I looked around and literally seen millions and millions of people for thousands of miles in every direction floating towards the same light. Now I was thinking, this must be a fucking alien invasion! I started screaming. I've seen way too many movies to go out like this. I tried to get other people's attention but, they were just floating all happy and shit. I figured they were reliving their life's best moments, like I had earlier. My efforts were useless. I yelled for hours at the top of my lungs hoping that someone snapped out of this mass trance. After continuous screaming I heard a voice.

"WHY!"

It was the deepest voice I'd ever heard. It was like James Earl Jones' voice times a hundred, in 5.1 Dolby Digital surround sound, connected to half a million 18 inch subwoofers. Basically, it was the most intimidating voice I'd ever heard but, at the same time it was somehow soothing.

I replied to the voice's question, with a question. "Why?!? Why the hell are you taking all these people?"

The voice replied, "The Hell is exactly why."

I was confused as shit.

The voice then said, "My child, you have lived your life as it was meant to be. For this I give you rapture to heaven. All the people you see here will have eternal life in my kingdom."

I was at a loss for words. The only thing I could say was, "Holy Shit". I looked around then said, "My bad, I didn't mean to curse."

The voice replied, "Words only have the power men give them."

In other words, he was saying its cool don't worry about it. He was just saying it all profound and what not. I was all kind of surprise. I mean, I'm a good dude but, I didn't think I would actually make it to heaven. I just saying, I did a lot of dirt in my day.

I was the only one not in a trance so, I just observed other people enjoy themselves. Then, I started to recognize people I knew. Family, friends, people I grew up with, and some dudes I worked with. I started thinking, how the hell did these motherfuckers get up here? I know for a fact my cousin sold dope his whole life and this nigga I work with has two kids that he doesn't claim! I started to see people that looked shady, grimy and downright ruthless.

I called out, "Hey! You just let anybody come to heaven? I'm seeing a lot of people that look messed up in the head floating to the light with me. I don't know if you overlooked them or not so, I'm just giving you a heads up."

The voice replied, "One genuine good deed outweighs a lifetime of desolation."

I said, "Word? So what happens now?"

"Now Jesus Christ will return and wage a 7 year war against the Antichrist. He will assemble an army of those that remain in the physical plane. Then he will defeat the antichrist in the final battle of Armageddon."

I shrugged my shoulders. "Sound good to me, sorry for questioning you."

As I'm getting closer to the light I thought, man that has to suck for Jesus. He literally has to create an army from the scum of the earth. I mean these guys were the worse of the worse if they were left behind right? Everybody was coming to heaven. I started to feel bad.

I finally reached the light and the voice said, "Do you accept rapture and your place in my kingdom?"

I sighed, "Nah man, send me back."

The voice deepened, "What? I offer you a place in my kingdom and you turn it down?"

"Nah, I appreciate it. As a matter of fact, you can hold on to it for me and I'll come get it in about 7 years or so. Just let me go help Jesus real quick and I'll be back."

The voice said, "You would give up eternal paradise, streets of gold, and 42 virgins for 7 years of torture, despair, and Hell on earth to help Jesus?"

I replied, "Word? 42 virgins? For real? Them niggas really had that shit right huh?"

The voice said, "What are you talking about?"

"Uh nothing, never mind. Look Sir, all I'm saying is that Jesus won't have anyone he can trust out there. Remember the last dudes that had his back? They just let him die. They didn't put up a fight or nothing. Imma ride for my dawg."

The voice laughed then said, "Free will, never fails to amaze me."

I laughed along with him, "If you could hook me up with some superman type powers that would be cool as a fan."

It didn't happen. I blinked then woke up in my bed. A dream?!? You gotta be shitting me. Damn, how much did I drink last night? Then, I heard loud Boom! I looked out of my window. Women were being raped, people were looting, and balls of fire were falling from the sky. Damn, I guess it wasn't a dream. How long had I been gone for all of this to have happened? I didn't know but, I knew I had to find Jesus. I began my search.

I traveled the underworld looking for any sign of where I might find him. It was worse than any movie could ever capture. People bartered water for body parts. I was soon captured by a group of inbreed hillbillies. They also captured a younger black woman. They made us have sex with each other while they licked us and pissed on us. It was the most degrading thing I'd ever been forced to do. It appeared that I had failed. It looked like I would die here.

It was very clear these people ate other people to survive. They ate in front of me and the girl. The food they ate was clearly cooked human parts. I could see distinguishable fingers and toes. After weeks of defilement, I could take no more.

I screamed, "You sick Fucks! You're fucking disgusting. You make us have sex just so you can get off."

They all laughed. Then the girl, who hadn't made a sound since the first time we met, started to cry uncontrollable tears.

The apparent leader of the redneck group said, "You're not fucking so we can get off, you're fucking so we can eat!" Then, they all laughed again.

The girl cried more. I asked her, "What do they mean?

In the weakest voice I'd ever heard, she mumbled, "They plan to get me pregnant then, when I'm close to having the baby, feast on my unborn child and my heavyset, pregnant body. You'll be dead as soon as they think I'm pregnant."

Different tone in these pages right now but, I must capture how cruel "Hell" on earth really is. I cried myself to sleep that night then, I heard gunshots. My room door swung open and my barely conscious, food and water deprived body was picked up and hauled off.   When I awoke, Jesus stood over me.

He said, "My Father told me you came to help me win this war."

 I asked him, "How did you know where I was?"

 "When you came back for me, you created a bond. I will always know where you are."

I told Jesus, "You mean to tell me you knew exactly where I was this whole damn time and you took this fucking long to come get me? You know they had me eating rats and shit!"

He looked at me perplexed, "Mother Fucka, you lucky I came got yo ass at all. Nigga I walked here, from Egypt, on water, looking for yo dumb ass. I didn't need yo help. I'm Jesus Fucking Christ! Please say the Christ!"

Pause, y'all probably saying, Jesus didn't talk like that. Bullshit, I was there and Jesus was hood. Un-Pause.

He said, "Stop crying and drink this water."

With a bit of sarcasm I demanded, "You better turn that water into some Henny. I been locked up for weeks, I need a shot." And wouldn't you know it; he turned that shit into a glass of the best cognac I'd ever drank. We got tipsy as hell. Well, I guess at this point, you can say Earth since hell was now on Earth. So, I rephrase that. We got tipsy as "Earth" that night and so began our friendship and hunt for the antichrist.

JC was cool as the other side of the pillow. Oh, I called him JC since we got all cool and shit. If this was a movie, there would be a montage right here. It would show me and JC training together, taking names, kicking ass, and just fucking demons up in the name of the lord. Unfortunately, this is a book so I'm supposed to say something like, "Over the next few years JC and I grew closer." Well, damn that! That's not how it's going down! Close your eyes and imagine the Matrix (Part 1) meets Die Hard mixed with a dash of Harry Potter because, JC was always doing some David Blaine type shit, then add that to every Karate movie ever made and a pinch of the Holy Ghost. POW! That's what the next 5 years were like.

JC and I were as thick as thieves. Yeah sure, he was pretty cool with everyone else in his army too but, this ain't about them. This is about me! I was closer anyway. For example, I remember one battle. We were fighting these little demon midgets. Don't laugh because they were midgets, these little fuckers were evil! They would dip the tips of their arrows in poison and demolish full cities. Ok, I'm lying. They weren't that much of a challenge. We kicked their ass pretty easy. It wasn't the hardest battle of the war. In fact, I think it was the easiest to be honest but, thats neither here nor there. Pause! Where the "Earth" did that saying come from? Neither here nor there. Dumbest shit ever. Anyway, back to the story. We were kicking those little Ommpa Lumpa's asses then, one of them got a lucky shot in on JC. The little guy knocked JC down to his knees then, Bam! Arrow, dead in the ass!

I laughed, "Damn JC, you can walk on water but you can't beat a guy 3 foot nothing. You be dodging bullets and shit like you in a movie and you can't block a punch from a itty bitty little midget hand? You lookin' like a real bitch right now."

JC said, "Screw you. Think about what name every girl you ever been with has called out. That's right nigga, Jesus!"

"Whatever, you still got your ass whipped by a midget.

JC suddenly stopped laughing. "Rafael."

Ok, let me explain something I forgot to mention. JC had this divine tone of voice he would use when he wasn't joking. He was using this tone now so, I knew something was wrong.

I replied, "What's good JC, everything straight?"

"I think that arrow was poisoned. I can stop the spreading but, you're gonna have to suck the poison out."

Quickly I said, "I'm not sucking nothing. Let me go grab somebody."

"There's no time, you have to do it now or I will die and all will be lost."

I looked at him stupid. "I'm not sucking on your ass man. That's not how we get down."

JC sighed, "Man I died for your sins, remember that."

I said, "Nigga that shit was years ago. Can't you just heal yourself or something?"

"No fool, it don't work like that. Don't you think I would have done that shit on the cross?"

Pause! Speaking of the cross, JC didn't really like that it was plastered everywhere. I mean think about it, would you want reminders of the most horrific thing that ever happened to you hanging on every wall in world? I think not. Ok, un-Pause.

I leaned in and sucked the poison out of JC's left butt cheek.

JC started laughing uncontrollably. "Gotcha! That arrow wasn't poisoned. I just made you kiss my ass. Those that cross me shall be punished. HaHaHaHa!!!" Then he said, "That's what you get for calling me a bitch."

I said, "Words only have as much power as man give them."

"Where'd you here that dumb shit?" JC said.

"From yo daddy. He told me that before I came down here to help yo simple ass." We didn't speak again for two weeks.

We'd been searching for the Antichrist for over 5 years. I really had no concept of time. I was just estimating. Finally, we found where he was hiding at. We devised a tactical extraction plan. Three men would go in back, two through the roof, snipers would take position a few meters away and JC would take point on the extraction, kicking in the main door. Oh buddy, the shit was about to hit the proverbial fan! All of a sudden, bombs rained on us from above. Gun shots came from all angles. Someone had given us up.

I screamed, "JC, somebody betrayed us!"

JC sighed. "It was Derrick. I knew it would happen yesterday when we were eating chow."

I was furious, "Man why didn't you tell me! This is the second time you done did this shit! Didn't you learn your lesson two thousand years ago with Judas bitch ass?"

JC laughed, "Free will bruh, you can't fuck with it."

I was pissed. But, I still fought alongside my dawg like there was no tomorrow. Well technically, if this was Armageddon, there was no tomorrow. I cleared a path for JC to enter the compound and capture the Anti-Christ. Then, he went rouge. Shortly after, I took a bullet to the brain. I opened my eyes and I was in the most beautiful place I've ever seen. All the descriptions of Heaven never came close. No one ever mentions the Aroma. It smells like, wait.... I don't want to give it away. You'll see if you make it there. Anyway, I woke up in heaven. Clearly, I died on the battle field.

I screamed, "Send me back!"

A voice said, "No, only he can defeat the Anti-Christ."

Oh shit, it was that deep ass, James Earl Jones voice again. This time, I didn't argue. I sat my black ass down, feeling useless. After about 30 minutes, trumpets blew, the gates of Heaven swung open, and the soldiers returned home. I still don't know what went on down there after I died but, the smile JC had on his face told me I never had to worry about anything like that again. JC and I would see each other in passing but, never really hung out much after the war. He was a busy man and I spun most of my time with my 10,000 family members from generations past. I barely seen JC over the next few eons but, I always felt the bond we created back on Earth. When the younger generations speak of the Seven Year War, I can't help but to remember that crazy bastard and all the good times we had.

The End!

ABOUT THE AUTHOR

RAFAEL WILLIAMS: Rafael is a damn good person. He never fucked over anybody that didn't have it coming. Ok, here is the real. Rafael is the mother fucking man. He has had sex with well over 100 women and at least 75 of them are what niggas consider, BAD BITCHES! He was born in a little town called Crowley in Louisiana. At age 18 he ventured off into the world to make his mark. He has accomplished that shit at least 20 times. The irony is, he really wants a woman to settle down with but, his reputation will not allow it. The movies, "Good Luck Chuck" and "How to Be A Player" are loosely based on his life. He can win a game of Tic-Tac-Toe in one move. He once slammed a revolving door. As a kid, everyone wore Superman PJs. Well, Superman wore

Rafael PJs. Rafael has to tuck his dick in his boots (It's that big). What we are trying to say is, he is WINNING so get your shit together and get like him!

www.ingramcontent.com/pod-product-compliance
Lightning Source LLC
Chambersburg PA
CBHW032005040426
42448CB00006B/483